D1207477

The Hardy Boyz

Pro Wrestlers Matt and Jeff Hardy

by Angie Peterson Kaelberer

Reading Consultant:
Dr. Robert Miller
Professor of Special Education
Minnesota State University, Mankato

CAPSTONE
HIGH-INTEREST
BOOKS

an imprint of Capstone Press
Mankato, Minnesota

Capstone High-Interest Books are published by Capstone Press
151 Good Counsel Drive, P.O. Box 669, Mankato, Minnesota 56002
http://www.capstone-press.com

Library of Congress Cataloging-in-Publication Data
Kaelberer, Angie Peterson.
    The Hardy Boyz: pro wrestlers Matt and Jeff Hardy / by Angie Peterson
Kaelberer.
    p. cm.—(Pro wrestlers)
    Summary: Traces the lives and careers of professional wrestlers and brothers
Matt and Jeff Hardy, who have succeeded both individually and as the tag team
known as the Hardy Boyz.
    Includes bibliographical references and index.
    ISBN 0-7368-2142-2
    1. Hardy, Matt, 1973 or 4– —Juvenile literature. 2. Hardy, Jeff—Juvenile
literature. 3. Hardy Boyz (Wrestlers)—Juvenile literature. 4. Wrestlers—United
States—Biography—Juvenile literature. [1. Hardy, Matt, 1973 or 4– 2. Hardy, Jeff.
3. Hardy Boyz (Wrestlers) 4. Wrestlers.] I. Title. II. Series.
GV1196.A1K34 2004
796.812'092'2—dc21   2003006439

Editorial Credits
Karen Risch, product planning editor; Timothy Halldin, series designer;
    Patrick Dentinger, book designer; Jo Miller, photo researcher

Photo Credits
Dr. Michael Lano, 10 (both), 13, 14, 17, 25, 26, 29 (left), 33, 34
Michael Blair, cover (all), 4, 7, 18, 21, 22, 29 (right), 30, 36, 39, 40, 42 (both)

1 2 3 4 5 6 08 07 06 05 04 03

Capstone Press thanks Dr. Michael Lano, WReaLano@aol.com, for his assistance in the
preparation of this book.

Table of Contents

Chapter 1

Hometown Champions

On June 29, 1999, pro wrestling fans filled the Crown Coliseum in Fayetteville, North Carolina. The fans were there to see the wrestlers of the World Wrestling Federation (WWF) perform.

Many of the Fayetteville fans were there to see the Hardy Boyz tag team. Brothers Matt and Jeff Hardy grew up in Cameron, North Carolina. This town is about 30 miles (48 kilometers) from Fayetteville.

Matt is the older of the Hardy Boyz and usually acted as the team's leader.

A Championship Match

That night, Matt and Jeff had a chance to win the WWF World Tag Team title from the Acolytes. The Acolytes were Ron Simmons, who wrestles as Farooq, and John Hayfield, known as Bradshaw.

Matt and Jeff walked to the ring with their manager, Michael Seitz. Seitz wrestled as Michael Hayes. Hayes leaned on a cane as he walked.

To start the match, Matt climbed to the top rope. He jumped down on Farooq and Bradshaw. Instead of falling, the Acolytes caught Matt. Jeff then did a somersault off the top rope, taking all three men down. Bradshaw threw Jeff out of the ring as Matt battled Farooq inside the ring. Jeff jumped in the ring, and Farooq took him down with a powerslam.

Farooq tagged Bradshaw, who kicked Matt. Both Acolytes threw Matt into a corner of the ring. Matt got up on the top rope. He jumped down on Bradshaw, but Bradshaw caught him. Jeff stood on the ring's apron and dropkicked Bradshaw to the middle of the ring. Matt then

Jeff hoped to win his first WWF title in his home state.

tried to cover Bradshaw for the pin, but
Bradshaw kicked out.

Later in the match, Hayes jumped up on the
apron. Farooq jumped out of the ring and
attacked Hayes. The referee tried to break up
Farooq and Hayes. Jeff picked up Hayes' cane
and hit Bradshaw over the head. Matt then took
Bradshaw down with a tornado DDT. Matt
put Bradshaw in a front facelock. Matt then

jumped around Bradshaw as he sent Bradshaw crashing to the mat.

The referee turned back to the action in the ring as Matt covered Bradshaw for the pin. The referee counted to three. Matt and Jeff had won their first WWF title in front of many of their friends and family members.

About the Hardy Boyz

Matt Hardy is 6 feet, 2 inches (188 centimeters) tall and weighs 225 pounds (102 kilograms). His younger brother Jeff is the same height, but weighs 215 pounds (98 kilograms). Matt and Jeff have been wrestling since they were teenagers in North Carolina. They turned pro in 1993 and joined the WWF in 1998. This company is now called World Wrestling Entertainment (WWE).

As a tag team, Matt and Jeff won five WWF Tag Team Championships. They also won the World Championship Wrestling (WCW) Tag Team title after the WWF bought WCW in April 2001.

Early in 2002, Matt and Jeff began competing in singles matches. They have both won several singles titles.

Major Matches

June 29, 1999—Matt and Jeff defeat the Acolytes to win their first WWF Tag Team title.

March 5, 2001—Matt and Jeff defeat the Dudley Boyz to win their fourth WWF Tag Team title.

April 10, 2001—Jeff defeats Triple H to win the WWF Intercontinental Championship.

April 24, 2001—Matt becomes the WWF European Champion by defeating Eddy Guerrero.

July 10, 2001—Jeff defeats Mike Awesome for the WWF Hardcore Championship.

October 8, 2001—Jeff and Matt defeat Test and Booker T to win the WCW World Tag Team title.

November 12, 2001—Matt and Jeff win their fifth WWF Tag Team title by defeating Booker T and Test.

July 8, 2002—Jeff defeats William Regal to become the WWF European Champion.

February 23, 2003—Matt defeats Billy Kidman to win the WWE Cruiserweight title.

Chapter 2

The Early Years

Matthew Moore Hardy was born September 23, 1974, in Cameron, North Carolina. Jeffrey Nero Hardy was born August 31, 1977, in Cameron. Jeff and Matt's father is Gilbert. Their mother's name was Ruby.

The Hardy family lived on a farm near Cameron. Gilbert raised tobacco and worked for the U.S. Postal Service. Jeff and Matt spent many hours helping their father in the tobacco fields. They also found time to have fun. Both boys played football and baseball. Jeff also raced dirt bikes.

In 1986, Ruby became sick with cancer and died. Matt was 12 years old and Jeff was 9.

Matt and Jeff were born and grew up in Cameron, North Carolina.

Their mother's death was very hard for the boys. Matt and Jeff had always been close, but they became even closer after Ruby died.

Wrestling Fans

As children, Matt and Jeff watched pro wrestling on TV. They were fans of both the WWF and the National Wrestling Alliance (NWA). This wrestling company was based in Atlanta, Georgia.

In 1987, Gilbert gave Jeff and Matt a trampoline. The boys put the trampoline in their backyard and turned it into a wrestling ring. They cut down four small trees for the ringposts. They strung garden hoses on the posts for ropes.

Matt and Jeff invited their friends over to wrestle. The boys tried to copy the moves of their favorite pro wrestlers. They made championship belts out of cardboard. They even rented video cameras to film their matches.

Today, Matt and Jeff say that wrestling in their backyard was very dangerous. They and their friends were lucky not to have been seriously hurt.

The Hardy Boyz's Heroes: The Fabulous Freebirds

Michael Hayes

The Fabulous Freebirds were Michael Hayes, Terry Gordy, and Buddy Jack Roberts. Hayes and Gordy formed the team in 1979. Roberts joined the Freebirds in 1980.

Most tag teams have only two members. With three members, the Freebirds had an advantage. During the 1980s, the team won titles in Georgia Championship Wrestling and World Class Championship Wrestling. Roberts later retired. Jimmy Garvin replaced him. In June 1989, the Freebirds won the NWA World Tag Team title. Soon after, Gordy left the team. In 1991, Hayes and Garvin won the WCW World Tag Team title.

Today, Hayes and Garvin are retired from active wrestling. Gordy died in 2001.

Matt and Jeff always hoped to wrestle for the WWF.

Teenage Years

Matt and Jeff attended Union Pines High School in Cameron. Both boys played football for the Union Pines Vikings. Jeff also wrestled on the school's team.

During high school, Matt and Jeff stayed interested in pro wrestling. They replaced their homemade ring with a real wrestling ring. They practiced every day. Soon, the boys were wrestling at shows at county fairs all over North Carolina. They formed their own wrestling company, the Teenage Wrestling Federation. Later, they changed the company's name to the East Coast Wrestling Federation.

In 1992, Matt graduated from Union Pines. He started classes at the University of North Carolina-Charlotte. Matt planned to get a degree in engineering, but he had not forgotten about wrestling. He and Jeff still hoped to wrestle for the WWF.

Chance at the Big Time
At a wrestling show, Matt and Jeff met a wrestler known as the Italian Stallion. The Stallion hired Matt and Jeff to wrestle matches in North Carolina for the Professional Wrestling Federation (PWF).

In 1993, the Stallion asked Matt and Jeff to wrestle in a WWF match. WWF wrestlers had to be at least 18 years old. Matt was 19, but Jeff was only 16. Jeff told WWF officials that he was 18.

After a few WWF matches, both Matt and Jeff wrestled on the WWF TV show *Raw Is War.* Matt wrestled Nikolai Volkoff.

Jeff wrestled Scott Hall. Matt and Jeff did not win their matches, but they were excited to be in the ring with top WWF wrestlers.

In summer 1994, Gilbert became sick from a blood clot in his brain. Instead of returning to college, Matt stayed home to look after him. After Gilbert got better, Matt began classes at Sandhills Community College in the nearby town of Pinehurst.

OMEGA

In 1997, Matt and Jeff changed their company's name to the Organization of Modern Extreme Grappling Arts (OMEGA). They hired seven other wrestlers to compete in OMEGA matches.

Matt and Jeff were in charge of every part of OMEGA. They made posters, sold tickets, and set up rings for each show. Matt even made wrestling costumes for himself and Jeff.

In OMEGA, Matt and Jeff developed the signature moves they would later use in the WWF. Jeff started using the Swanton Bomb. During this move, Jeff stands on the top rope and arches his back as he does a backward somersault onto his opponent. Matt created the Twist of Fate. For this move, Matt puts his

Jeff later used the Swanton Bomb in the WWF.

opponent in a front facelock. He puts his arm underneath the opponent's neck as he jumps in the air. He then slams the opponent's head against the mat.

Matt and Jeff continued to run OMEGA while wrestling a WWF show every few months. In April 1998, WWF officials asked Matt and Jeff to sign a contract. Their dream of wrestling for the world's largest pro wrestling company was about to come true.

Chapter 3

The WWF

In August 1998, the WWF sent Matt and Jeff to its training camp in Stamford, Connecticut. At the camp, Matt and Jeff trained every day. They practiced new moves and learned how to make TV promos.

On September 27, 1998, Matt and Jeff wrestled as the Hardy Boyz for the first time on WWF TV. They defeated Mens Teoh and Sho Funaki, who wrestled as Kaientai.

Breaking into the WWF

After winning their first match, Matt and Jeff's luck changed. For months, they lost nearly all of their matches. In spring 1999,

In 1998, Matt's dream of joining the WWF came true.

We had a tough journey [into the wrestling business], but any journey that is tough can be rewarding.
—Matt Hardy, 1Wrestling.com, 3/28/03

WWF officials decided the Hardy Boyz needed some help. They asked Michael Hayes to manage Matt and Jeff. In the 1980s, Hayes had been a member of the Fabulous Freebirds. As teenagers, Matt and Jeff often copied the moves of this tag team.

Hayes helped Matt and Jeff in several ways. He showed them better ways to put their moves together. He also helped them become more confident in the ring.

Hayes' help paid off for Matt and Jeff. In June, the brothers won their first WWF title when they defeated tag team champions the Acolytes. At 24 and 21, Matt and Jeff were the youngest wrestlers to ever win this title. They held the title for less than a month before losing it to the Acolytes.

After losing the title, Matt and Jeff decided to leave Hayes. They started looking for a new manager.

Jeff and Matt do many of their moves off the ropes.

A High-Flying Team

Matt and Jeff had a different style than most wrestlers. They performed many of their moves off the top rope or the ringpost. They also did well in cage matches and ladder matches. Fans started to cheer for Jeff and Matt. They waited

to see what daring moves the brothers would do next.

In fall 1999, Jeff and Matt began a series of matches with Adam Copeland and Jason Reso. Copeland wrestles as Edge, while Reso is known as Christian. Manager Terri Runnels set up the matches. She said she would manage the team that won three out of five matches. By October 14, each team had won two matches. The next match would decide the winner.

Match of the Year

On October 17, 1999, the wrestlers came to Cleveland, Ohio, for the WWF's No Mercy event. At No Mercy, Jeff and Matt would face Edge and Christian in the last match of their best-of-five series.

The No Mercy match was a ladder match. WWF workers had hung a bag from the arena's ceiling. Inside the bag was $100,000 in cash. Two ladders lay by the ring. The first wrestler to climb a ladder and grab the bag would keep

The No Mercy match was a ladder match.

> What we did that night in the tag team ladder match was historic and can never be duplicated or relived.
> —Matt Hardy, WWFHardys.com, 1999

the money for his team. The winning team also would have Runnels as its manager.

Late in the match, the four wrestlers were all battling inside the ring. One 8-foot (2.4-meter) ladder was set up in a corner of the ring. The other was folded and lay across the upright ladder like a seesaw. Jeff jumped from the top rope and landed on one end of the ladder. The other end of the ladder rose up and hit Edge and Christian, knocking them to the mat.

The wrestlers then set up each ladder in the ring. Matt and Edge climbed up one ladder. Jeff and Christian climbed up the other. Edge shoved Matt into the ropes. As Matt fell, he took down the other ladder. Christian fell to the mat, but Jeff jumped over onto the other ladder.

Jeff and Edge started climbing the ladder. As they reached the top, Jeff pushed Edge away and grabbed the sack of money as he fell to the mat. The Hardys had won $100,000 and a new manager.

Edge and Christian were Jeff and Matt's opponents in many of their best tag team matches.

Wrestling fans enjoyed the exciting ladder match. The fans voted it the match of the year on the WWF's Internet site. The next night, fans stood and cheered for Jeff and Matt as they walked into the ring. The brothers had become wrestling superstars.

Chapter 4

Team Extreme

In February 2000, Amy Dumas joined the WWF. Dumas wrestles as Lita. She had become friends with Matt and Jeff when they ran OMEGA in North Carolina.

At first, Lita worked as a valet for Jesús Saldaña, who wrestled as Essa Rios. Valets walk to the ring with wrestlers. The valets cheer for the wrestlers and try to help them win their matches. Lita later began wrestling on her own.

In May 2000, Lita teamed with Matt and Jeff. She was a strong wrestler who often helped them win matches. Matt, Jeff, and Lita were all in their early 20s. In the ring, they

Lita teamed with the Hardy Boyz in 2000.

I am who I am. I can't help it if other people aren't as comfortable in their own skin.—Jeff Hardy, *The Hardy Boyz: Exist 2 Inspire*, 3/03

wore mesh shirts and baggy pants. Jeff and Lita had body piercings and tattoos. Jeff also painted his fingernails and dyed his hair blue, red, and other colors. Wrestling fans started to call them Team Extreme.

On August 27, 2000, Matt and Jeff wrestled in the first Tables, Ladders, and Chairs (TLC) match. Edge, Christian, Mark Lomonica, and Devon Hughes also wrestled in this match. Lomonica is known as Bubba Ray Dudley in the ring. Hughes is D-Von Dudley. Together, they wrestle as the Dudley Boyz. Edge and Christian won the TLC match.

Champions Again

In September 2000, Matt and Jeff challenged Edge and Christian to a title match. The match was a cage match. All four wrestlers were locked into a steel cage that covered the ring. Ladders and chairs were near the ring. The first wrestler who climbed out of the opening

Bubba Ray Dudley

D-Von Dudley

Matt and Jeff had many of their greatest tag team matches against the Dudley Boyz. Mark Lomonica wrestles as Bubba Ray Dudley. Devon Hughes is D-Von Dudley.

Both Bubba Ray and D-Von began wrestling in the early 1990s. In 1996, they teamed in Extreme Championship Wrestling (ECW). In 2000, Bubba Ray and D-Von joined the WWF as the Dudley Boyz. Between 2000 and 2002, they won six WWF Tag Team titles. In 2002, they split to compete in singles matches. Late in 2002, Bubba Ray and D-Von joined to compete as the Dudley Boyz again. In early 2003, they won the WWE Tag Team title.

Jeff climbed to the top of the cage as he prepared to do a moonsault.

at the top of the cage and down to the floor would win the title for his team.

Early in the match, Jeff climbed to the top of the cage. Edge climbed after Jeff and threw him out of the cage to the floor. Edge and Christian both attacked Matt as he climbed to the top of the cage. Matt tried to climb out, but

Edge and Christian threw him to the mat. Christian climbed out of the cage. Jeff threw a ladder at Christian's head, knocking him to the floor.

Jeff climbed back into the cage and did a backward somersault. Jeff's moonsault knocked both Matt and Edge to the mat. Edge got up and hit Jeff with a chair. Edge then started climbing the cage. Matt and Jeff each grabbed a folding chair and followed Edge. At the top of the cage, Matt and Jeff hit Edge with the chairs at the same time. Edge fell straight back off the top of the cage. Matt and Jeff climbed down the cage. They were the new WWF Tag Team Champions.

Matt and Jeff held the title until October 22, when they lost it to Edge and Christian at No Mercy in Albany, New York. The next night, Matt and Jeff won the title back in Hartford, Connecticut. They kept the title until November 6, when they lost to Charles Wright and Barry "Bull" Buchanan. Wright wrestled as the Goodfather. On March 5, 2001, Matt and Jeff defeated the Dudley Boyz to win their fourth WWF Tag Team title.

More Tables, Ladders, and Chairs

On April 1, 2001, Matt and Jeff prepared to defend their title at pro wrestling's biggest event, WrestleMania. They would wrestle the Dudley Boyz, Edge, and Christian in a TLC match.

Before the match, WWF workers hung the Tag Team belts from the arena's ceiling. They also placed tables, ladders, and folding chairs near the ring's entrance. The first tag team to climb a ladder and grab the belts would win.

Each team had another wrestler at ringside to help them. Lita walked to the ring with Matt and Jeff. Matthew Hyson, who wrestles as Spike Dudley, was with the Dudley Boyz. Terry Gerin came to the ring with Edge and Christian. Gerin wrestles as Rhyno.

During the match, the wrestlers knocked each other off ladders, hit each other with chairs, and slammed each other through tables. At the end of the match, Bubba Ray Dudley and Matt climbed a tall ladder to the ceiling.

Christian tried to stop Jeff from grabbing the belt from the ceiling.

Test was one of Matt and Jeff's opponents during two Tag Team title matches in 2001.

Rhyno shook Matt and Bubba off the ladder, sending them crashing onto the tables below. Rhyno climbed the ladder with Christian on his shoulders. Christian grabbed the belts to win the championship.

Like the first TLC match, this match was popular with wrestling fans. They voted it the match of the year on the WWF's Internet site.

More Championships

After losing the title at WrestleMania, Matt and Jeff competed in a few singles matches. In April 2001, Jeff became the Intercontinental Champion and Matt won the European title. That summer, Jeff won the Hardcore Championship twice. He also won the Light Heavyweight title.

In fall 2001, Matt and Jeff won two more tag team titles. On October 8, Matt and Jeff defeated Booker Huffman and Andrew Martin for the WCW Tag Team title. Huffman wrestles as Booker T and Martin is Test. The next month, Matt and Jeff defeated Booker T and Test to win the WWF Tag Team Championship.

On December 9, Matt and Jeff wrestled against each other for the first time in the WWF. Jeff took down Matt with a Swanton Bomb to win the match.

Chapter 5

The Hardy Boyz Today

Early in 2002, Matt and Jeff decided they had reached every goal they set for themselves as a tag team. They wanted to see what they could each do on their own.

The brothers wanted to wrestle together one more time. On March 17, 2002, Matt and Jeff wrestled as a team at WrestleMania. They competed in a four-way tag team match against the Acolytes, the Dudley Boyz, and champions Monty Sopt and Chuck Palumbo. Sopt wrestles as Billy Gunn.

By 2002, the Hardy Boyz had reached all of their goals, including winning the WCW Tag Team title.

Gunn and Palumbo won the match and kept the title. After WrestleMania, Matt and Jeff split to compete in singles events.

On Their Own

On March 25, the WWF split its wrestlers into two groups. One group appeared only on *Raw*. The other group appeared only on *Smackdown!* Matt became part of the *Smackdown!* group, while Jeff competed on *Raw*.

Matt and Jeff continued to compete in singles matches. On July 8, 2002, Jeff defeated Darren Matthews to become the European Champion. Matthews wrestles as William Regal. Later that month, Jeff won the Hardcore Championship from Bradshaw. In February 2003, Matt defeated Peter Gruner to win the Cruiserweight title. Gruner wrestles as Billy Kidman.

Outside the Ring

Matt and Jeff have both built houses near their father's home. When they are not traveling, they spend time with their father and other family and friends in Cameron.

Jeff and Matt wrestled Billy Gunn, Chuck Palumbo, and the Dudley Boyz at WrestleMania 18.

Matt and Jeff enjoy meeting their fans. They often visit sick children in hospitals and speak to groups of children at schools.

Of the two brothers, Matt is more focused on wrestling. Jeff has many interests outside of wrestling. He draws, paints, and writes poetry

Jeff's wrestling injuries may force him to retire early.

and songs. He also plays guitar with a band called Peroxwhy?gen (purr-AWK-suh-juhn).

Matt and Jeff have appeared on TV shows. In 1999, they played wrestlers on *That '70s Show*. In 2002, Matt, Jeff, and Lita appeared with three other wrestlers on *Fear Factor*. On this show, people compete by performing

I have slowed down a lot of late and so has Matt. You can't do that [high-flying stunts] forever.
—Jeff Hardy, 1Wrestling.com, 3/28/03

daring stunts. Matt won the competition. He gave the $50,000 he won to the American Cancer Society. Matt hoped that the money would help people like his mother.

In March 2003, Matt and Jeff published their autobiography. This book about their lives is called *The Hardy Boyz: Exist 2 Inspire*.

The Future

Matt and Jeff still have career goals. They both hope to someday be the WWE World Champion. They may even wrestle as a team again.

Matt and Jeff's high-flying style of wrestling has caused them many injuries. Most wrestlers retire by age 40, but Matt and Jeff know they may have to quit wrestling before that age. Matt says he always wants to work in the wrestling business. Jeff says he will focus on music and art after his wrestling career is over.

Career Highlights

1974 — Matt is born September 23.

1977 — Jeff is born August 31.

1993 — Matt and Jeff start wrestling at WWF shows.

1997 — Matt and Jeff form OMEGA.

1998 — Matt and Jeff join the WWF.

1999 — Matt and Jeff win their first WWF Tag Team Championship.

2000 — Lita teams with Matt and Jeff; the brothers win their second WWF Tag Team title and also compete in the first TLC match.

2001 — Matt and Jeff win two more Tag Team titles and compete in the second TLC match; they both win several singles titles.

2002 — Matt and Jeff split up their tag team; Jeff wins the European and Hardcore Championships.

2003 — Matt becomes the WWE Cruiserweight Champion; the brothers publish an autobiography.

Words to Know

autobiography (aw-toh-bye-OG-ruh-fee)—a book in which the author tells the story of his or her life

cancer (KAN-sur)—a serious disease in which unhealthy cells in the body destroy healthy cells

contract (KON-trakt)—a legal agreement between a wrestler and a wrestling company

manager (MAN-uh-jur)—a person who is in charge of a wrestler's career

referee (ref-uh-REE)—a person who makes sure athletes follow the rules of a sport

signature move (SIG-nuh-chur MOOV)—the move for which a wrestler is best known; this move also is called a finishing move.

trampoline (TRAM-puh-leen)—a piece of canvas attached to a frame by elastic ropes or springs; people jump on trampolines.

valet (vah-LAY)—a person who walks to the ring with a wrestler and helps the wrestler during matches

To Learn More

Alexander, Kyle. *Women of Pro Wrestling.* Pro Wrestling Legends. Philadelphia: Chelsea House, 2001.

Hunter, Matt. *Pro Wrestling's Greatest Matches.* Pro Wrestling Legends. Philadelphia: Chelsea House, 2001.

Hunter, Matt. *Pro Wrestling's Greatest Tag Teams.* Pro Wrestling Legends. Philadelphia: Chelsea House, 2001.

Pope, Kristian, and Ray Whebbe Jr. *The Encyclopedia of Professional Wrestling: 100 Years of the Good, the Bad, and the Unforgettable.* Iola, Wis.: Krause Publications, 2001.

Useful Addresses

Professional Wrestling Hall of Fame
P.O. Box 434
Latham, NY 12110

World Wrestling Entertainment Inc.
1241 East Main Street
Stamford, CT 06902

Internet Sites

Do you want to learn more about the Hardy Boyz?
Visit the FactHound at *http://www.facthound.com*

FactHound can track down many sites to help you. All
the FactHound sites are hand-selected by our editors.
FactHound will fetch the best, most accurate information
to answer your questions.

IT'S EASY! IT'S FUN!
1) Go to *http://www.facthound.com*
2) Type in: 0736821422
3) Click on "FETCH IT" and FactHound will put you on
    the trail of several helpful links.

You can also search by subject or book title. So, relax
and let our pal FactHound do the research for you!

Index